SPECS OF SOCIETY

MAYANK RAMANI | NISARG PATIL

This book is dedicated to all the

supporting co-authors and readers.

Contents

Contents

Acknowledgements

We want to thanks team Notion Press
for providing such an amazing platform for authors !!

1. Mayank Ramani (publisher)

Mayank Ramani is a 16 years old diligent boy, positive thinker and a humble personality. He has fond of converting ideas into reality and now he is focusing on idea of creating a platform for deserving writers. You can appreciate his work on @confused_mayank/@dilse.shayar_ through Instagram.

Ignore Them

They will try to stop you
Ignore them !
They will try to break you
Ignore them !
They will laugh on your failure
Just ignore them
Whenever needed
Don't think why they cheated
Just ignore them
Whenever you feel like quitting
Just think to prove them wrong

Gather all your power
Cause your journey is long
Just ignore all the
Negative energy
You are not here
To make synergy
Just ignore them
And work on your dream
Their thinking is so lean !!

2. Nisarg Patil (compiler)

He is Nisarg Patil, He lives in Ambernath. He has a fond of literature. You can follow him on instagram- @unknown_nature2408/@nisargwrites.

The Society I See

The society I see,
Instead of living in harmony,
faces are now hiding jealousy,
which can lead to someone in agony.
Unity, bonding, togetherness is just
for the sake of knowledge in books,
in reality, world is getting into parts,
focusing on religion, casts and looks.
Failure is now
judged by grades,
the hardwork leaves behind,
and talent just fades.
There are still some real humans
apart from discrimination,
so are you a part of this mess of society,

SPECS OF SOCIETY

or are you the real one?

3. Rajeshwari Sinha

She is Rajeshwari Sinha . A graduate in Microbiology department and PGD in Hospital Management. Her write-ups have been featured in Elysian Magazine (September Edition 2021) and Doodly Minds Magazine (Jan Edition 2022). Living in Mumbai she has developed a peace for writings. She is a world hold record co-author. She hopes that her write-ups can connect with the readers reading her write-ups .She has given her writing contributions in 80 + anthologies and is a co-author in all of them. If anyone wants to read her write-ups they can follow The Unheard Stories on Instagram

Law Of Society

Human beings are a social animal
Gather as a families
Assemble as a group member
Congregate as supporters of association & parties.
Being in a socially formed member
People generalized all in the group
Along with one or two members

Who misbehave and act rough.
If father in the family is proven guilty of misconduct
He should be blame for is mischief;
Not name of the family, association & parties
Never generalized & underestimate all
is not the law of society.

4. Auwal Habeeb Abdulqadeer

He is Auwal Habeeb Abdulqadeer (Safana-The Poet). He has an imaginary kitchen where vowels and consonants are being cooked, A.K.A. Safana's Poetry Kitchen. He is a computer scientist, but playing with a pen is a passion and affectionate part of his life.

The Society In Me

We are born in
Yesterday and today
And tomorrow, we die in.
Here, where we rise to live.
Someday with blue and black.
Sometimes, a green atmosphere.
Sometimes, it's breathless.
Some are sleepless nights.
Some are sleeping at night.
It is where we endeavour.
To plant and harvest in.
With a brain and a hoe

It's our communal way.

a social society to live in.

It has a viable living alternative.

Our society can be bright.

Our society can be dark.

We vote for what is right.

Today and tomorrow, decided.

On the path to reaching the bright

On the path to reaching the dark.

We are unable to function.

in the absence of society.

And society is not functioning.

Without human endeavor,

Effectively, we are capable.

as in doer and don'ter.

Why can't a doer be uplifting?

And the don'ter be a doer?

We need to recall yesterday.

To make a beautiful day ahead

We need to deeply look into the sky.

To see the clouds, atmosphere, and stars

We need to look below our feet.

Will the sand make plants grow on it?

Our society is our home.

We live in, without a place to call home.

It affects our gestures and postures.

like breathing in and breathing out.

5. Binod Dawadi

Binod Dawadi, the author of The Power of Words, is a master's degree holder in Major English. He has worked on more than 1000 anthologies published in various renowned magazines. His vision is to change society through knowledge, so he wants to provide enlightenment to the people through his writing skills.

How Society Is Affecting Our Capabilities

Society accepts something,
From us but it doesn't know,
We are creating a dream as well as,
A mission in our life,
To read and to be the great man,
As well as after that serving our,
Society and making all happier,
But society can't have patience,
Society needs results at the present stage,
If we can't show our performance,
It do complaint and gossips,
By saying he is a useless man,

He can't do anything good,
For the society,
Neither he has done,
Anything good up to now,
Or he will do in the future,
In this way in the modern world,
All societies are materialist and selfish,
Un this way society is affecting our capabilities.

6. Ishita Banerjee

Born in January 2003 in kolkata , West Bengal studied till class 12 at St. Pauls boarding and day school, Kolkata.Currently pursuing BBA(Hospital Management) in NSHM Knowledge Campus, Kolkata . She has been writing poems ever since she was in class 6.Some of her works has also have been published in some local newspapers like The Telegraph(TTIS) and school magazines.Her poems have been featured in the book THE LAST FLOWER OF SPRING by Poem Pajama publications under Delhi Poerty Slam. "WHISPER OF HEARTS" by Bookfever publications and " MIRAKEE " by TGIWC.She also wants to write more in future and inspire all the sections of the society.

A Better Place

Through the half opened door
The vermillion liquid flowed
And covered the floor
Towards the edge lay her lifeless hand
Nothing was left to be said

Nothing was there to understand
Tears mixed with blood
What a pleasant sight
Too bad, she gave one of her own
Bones to others in their fights
Burnt her ownself to give others light
Gave her own food to the needy
And fed on poison at night
Yet endured the violence within her silence
Hope she is now in a better place
With a smile on her face

7. Mohanlal Majhi

Mohanlal Majhi from a small district of Odisha ,a boy named MOHANLAL MAJHI with dream and passion of writing ,willing to change the view of the society though his small poem. Voice of black/judgemental society

A little boy in black

A little boy in black,
born to slave.
Except outfit we hate black,
A boy in group being trolled,
A cat signs bad-luck,
A girl remain unmarried,
A night with horrific fiction.
Standing in queue with no one behind ,
Dreaming of bench, he got ground,
though with good brain he sit down,
sometime it hurts that why did I born,
Without mistake I proved wrong.

8. Sakshi Maurya

Sakshi Maurya a 16 year old self-supportive girl,positive thinker and full of enthusiasm.She is fond of reading books and listening music currently she is focusing on her studies as she want to pursue her dream of becoming a doctor you can follow her on @sakshimaurya808

We are enough!

Welcome to society,
Society tells us what to do
Get your masters degree,get married
We cannot fall in love because society repudiates
They bully us for smiling
Society shapes our opinion
But what we desire?
The need to build an empire
The empire of our own thoughts and opinions
A society where no one will interrupt our views
Society doesn`t defines us
We are the true definition
The definition of strength and perseverance

MAYANK RAMANI, NISARG PATIL

Because we are enough!!

9. Aditi Sharma

She is Aditi sharma . She is a college student at bhopal. She loves to spread positive quotes and make people smile . She is a poetryholic. She has been part of more than 35 anthologies. She loves to express herself to world through shayari,poetry , quotes etc She is a die- heart MSD and SSR FAN She loves to listen punjabi and old hindi songs . Her contents were also published in national and international newspapers.

Society

Society is a game
It only requires fame
Happening to be one among its member
Feels like being in a closed helpless chamber
Binding yourself with so-called rites and rules
Make you coward and among fools
Standard of it is pretty high
As if its valuable teaching like a sky
Seperation of population by caste is quite irrelavant
Even GOD would never thought this behaviour settlement

The happiness can be gained here
Relying on rites , justice never found here
Condition is just that you have to behave
deaf ,blind as act
You should be silent and minded react
All in one , the moral is
" NO MATTER WHAT SOCIETY PEOPLE DO ,
THEY SHOULD NOT BE BLAMED "

10. Nilofar Farooqui Tauseef

Nilofar Farooqui Tauseef, hails from Bihar Sharif, Nalanda but staying in Mumbai. She has done MCA & MBA. Team Leader by profession and writer by passion. She loves penning down her thoughts, emotions in her writing. For her "Pen is a sword to bring revolution". Her articles and research papers have been published in more than 300 books and magazines and in reputed journals of the country too.You can check her fb and instagram handled on- @writernilofar

Mirror of society

Education is a mirror of truth in society.
The symbol of greatness is the sandalwood surrounded by
arms.
If the country is fully developed.
To take women towards the progress of education.
Gives new shape economically and socially,
From knowledge to positive dreams come true.

Mother is the first teacher, she is the storehouse of
knowledge,
He is the supernatural incarnation of real and untrue.
From time immemorial, women were respected by acting,
Mirabai, Lakshmibai, Indira Gandhi became names.
Today's woman goes to office at home and outside too.
Step by step with the man, he also bears the expenses.
Connect the child to the new world, the mother is of the
future,
For women, education is a strong thread of progress.
By telling the story of the heroes, the heroic makes sons,
Education is priceless, it understands and tells.

11. Dr. Yusra khan

She is a medico-linguistic from Peshawar Pakistan. She is a story-teller, a poet, a blogger, a debator and social activist who is working on many national projects. Apart from medicine she is serving the community with their mental issues and personal issues, she's a counselor an artist and a published writer. She is an Ambassador of KP province for a female lead platform named Parwan-e-khanum. She loved to console people and providing solution to their problems. She is an English Editor of theauthorsattic which is an Anthology based program publishing Anthologies nationally and internationally. She's a source of motivation for many and avid participant of writing and recitation competitions held nationally and internationally. Hope you'll enjoy reading her mystic musings

Fuck the society Norms

Fuck the society Norms
Staying single as if tis' a sin
They throw stones of hatred

Of venom darts
Clipp off your wings
As you born not to fly
Educating women is a worthy action
But bullying and burning her peace
Mis-trusting and mis-interpreting her fierce soul
Gives societistical worm to spit out false facts
The worst society can do to harm a girl's peace
Focusing on early marriages
Depriving them from their basic rights
Dowry as most important job of parents
And prerequisite for groom's family
Fairness is the only known best complexion
Rest all out of league
Girls who work in offices, hospitals
Or any male dominated area
Are symbol of humiliation
To marry them would be ones absolute mistake
Working women/Earning birdie are stigmas
Blend of bad character and vulgar epithet
Society has abandon girls "future frame"
Imprison the delicate soul with her dreams in a cage
eternally.

12. B Raj Kumar

B Raj Kumar an electrical engineer by qualification has years of work experience spanning various industries. He wants to pursue his passion of writing poetry and novels in English as his 2nd career.

Why Society meetings?

We were just 8 flats in a complex,
We formed a society for all of us.
What should be the specs of this society?
When someone asked, I ran for my specs in a hurry.
We wanted to study and benchmark,
We 8 were a contrast in stark.
But then, we zeroed in on 2 of them,
Believe me, the unanimity in water supply and sewerage to stem.
In summer, we had to buy drinking water,
In winter, though it was a laughter.
We stopped conducting fortnightly society meeting,
We replaced it with chat, tea & snack eating.

13. Ishika Pawar

Ishika Pawar is an optimistic writer. Inspiring the readers through her writings is one of her ambitions. She holds an initiative to uplift or empower today's youth to make a constructive change in their lives.

Empower Yourself :Break the Shackles

How felt I when they ruptured me
into charred pieces of glass..
I thought of fitting their parameters,
branched off from my dreams to enhance..
Depression enveloping me,
They said,' Man up you can't be so weak!'
Realising everything is wrong here,
I crumbled down in tears..
I bowed no more ,elevated my thoughts
& became man with no fears..
I sheltered myself from humiliation,
self-pride inside me rolled away..

Valuing myself I walked away from toxicity which was
intolerable,
& unacceptable so as they!
Breaking these shackles,
To myself empower..
Focused on myself,
Inspirations to shower..

14. Alfita Afzal

Alfita from Allahabad is a passionate writer and loves to share her thoughts with others.She tries to convey her message with the best examples of life.

WHO'S RESPONSIBLE!

The last murder,did you remember.

Was on social media as a fantasy.

Is it the way to punish the guilty.

Now tell me whose responsible and Who should be.

It's the last rape case hope you know,

As was trend for days and weeks.

Will this lead to change the world?

It is only a world for online followers people need.

Now who's responsible !Who should be.

I am a girl, a pearl for family

How good it sounds to be!

But seems not that good for our community.

Just the thoughts of dowry, kill the girls of poor family.

Against something I would ask who's responsible! Who should be.

15. Kiran Pattnaik

This is Kiran Pattnaik, born and brought up in Sambalpur, Odisha. Pressure of studies and external factors attracted me towards writing, and listening. Whatever problem I face, the only medium I found to heal myself is to write about that topic. Just being a hobby, it changed to passion, and now to profession. The only thing you can limit yourself to, is time, because dreams has no limits, just like writing. You can add words and words; clauses and clauses; phrases and phrases; sentences and sentences and still it won't be enough. Because you can never express what you feel in some lines, there's always something extra, and that extra is what amazes the writers. "They paint the torn paper into a beautiful portrait of a human emotion". That is what I am - A Writer (Ræy).

Authority

Bring me back the choices
I made so far,
listening to the pleasant voices;

were someone's hidden scar.
I wonder what change does it make
to be a rebel,
Will I be a poisonous snake?
Or will I live in hell?
Tucking my hair,
covering my skin;
is it a part of your share
or a triumph of your win?
Being on a diet,
or a lady being chubby;
you taught me how to be quiet,
or else, I'll get a hubby.
Late night shifts
or a male friend,
I always receives a gift;
to make it end.
Dear civilized person,
Am I your maid?
My beat has gotten worsen
I need a little aid.
Not to get rights
or priority,
just a little twinkling lights,
and my soul's authority!

16. Anjali Jain

Anjali Jain loves to understand people and learn from them. A curious writer, her words are sword as well as shield. She always keeps on hunting for new opportunities & ways of life. You will be getting some amazing and creative content from her mind. She likes to write quotes, poems, research articles, blogs, basically everything as she says 'Bleeding Thoughts'. Learning & speaking different languages is her favorite task. Perfection in work is the only thing she wants! She quoted, "My hobby keeps on changing with time. Still exploring myself!" Instagram writer @a.j_moyotales

Society Norms, is it?

Why if n but to women?
Why 24x7 facility to men?
Why 100 pages rules for women?
Why not men?
Why 'bhul bhulaiya' life to women?

Why straight ways only to men?
Why so-called safety concern for women?
Why not men?
Why financial burden only on men?
Why household tantrums only on women?
Who's creating this endless dramatic circle?
Why?
Why?

17. K.S.Ramakrishnan

Mr.K.S.Ramakrishnan, Chennai doing his own business. He is agressive and go getter. His passion is writing. He participate in various competitions. He wish to excel in profession and passion.

Society

Amalgamation of an individuals are called society.

We are all lives in lovely society

It is our duty to take care of our society

Religion Caste Creed are evils in the society

Treat everyone as brother and sister in the society

Don't expect anything from the society

Have to reciprocate always to our society

Have we ever had been ro serve our society any point of time

?

When society makes me happy ?

Why don't I put my heart and soul for the society

From the bottom of my heart I love my society

18. Saswat Baral

Saswat Baral, Age 22, Born On August 20,1999 From Bhubaneswar, Odisha Co-Author Of 22 Anthologies, and a part of 3 Vajra World Records Anthology Projects. Passionate About: Writing, Cricket, Football, Kabbadi, Food, Travelling, Music And Public Speaking. Previously Attended Workshops Of MyCaptain: Stand Up Comedy And Humour Writing, Creative Writing, Novel Writing. Role Models: Rahul Dravid And Cristiano Ronaldo.

Nowadays,
A Student's Dignity Is Not Less Than A Bar Dancer's
People Throw Bundles Of Notes In Club,
To Watch Bar Dancers Dancing And Dance With Them
Too.
But The Bar Dancers Themselves Feel Compelled And
Suffocated.
And Hardly Those People Know They Are Wasting Their
Money For Momentary Pleasure.
Likewise,
People Sell Their Pants Off,
To Educate Their Child In Private Educational Institutions.

They Dance To The Tunes Of Private Institutions' Mentality
Of Snatching Money And Livelihood,
And Even They Make Their Kid Dance To It.
Hardly They Know, Their Kids Kill Their Dreams And
Ambitions For Them.
And Hardly They Know For Just A Momentary Happiness
Of Achieving That Piece Of Paper Called Certificate They
Are Knocking The Door Of Complex Situations Or Maybe
A Huge Loss Of Livelihood.
And The Most Common Thing In Bar Dancers And
Students Is That, They Were Compelled To Kill Their
Dreams And Get Exposed To The Atrocities Of The World,
And If They Complain To Their Respective People In Return
They Get Bangings. They Cry Alone Or Infront Of Few
People Whom They Trust Blindly.

19. Sangeeta Kumari

Sangeeta Kumari,She is a faculty of Political Science.Shd loves to write poems and stories.

Where is Humanity ?

Humanity is attached to human beings,
It's like a bond of love,
Sometimes humanity is selfish,
Humanity is no more an emotion for human being,
Humanity is divided in two phases,
One is Cruel,
And the second is innocent,
Hindu, Muslim, Sikh, Christian
Are all humans afterall,
Then why?
Why are we fighting to each other?
Why are we discriminating eachother?
All Holy books say,
Humanity is the key to Brotherhood,
God is one,
Then why are we fighting like cats & rats ?

We should respect all the religions..
Here many hearts are filled with sadness..
All waiting for happiness...
Sometimes I question, what is humanity ?
Where is humanity ?
Human being is a genius creature
Not to target anyone
But sometimes animals show their kindness & loyalty...
I respect all religions and humanity...
But where is humanity ?
Where is Humanity ?

20. Vijayamalathi Mani

Vijayamalathi Mani pursuing her Master Degree in English Literature. She is a poetess, co compiler, Compiler. She engrossed in inking quotes and poetry. She is a pluviophile.Glance her musings on YQ @Violet vibes. She wrote more than 3000 quotes on YQ. She has compiled 3 more anthologies. She received more than 250 e certificates in various competitions. She is the core member of Solaced pentales, World of Logophiles, Inner Souls. She has co-authored 500+ anthologies. She believes through writings only can win other's heart.

IS IT?

Is it?

Who said woman's life is easy?

Just take your hand and keep it to near your heart and tell the truth,

Can you ever live with a girl like mother, sister?

Can you ever observe them?

Are they leading a easy life?

There are many problems, sufferings, health issues etc.

But they make their heart and body strong,
And fight against it,
May be you think they are not get the job,
They just simply sit in the house,
And spend their time happily,
Is it?
They are doing every work in home,
Like cooking, cleaning, washing, mobbing, etc.
Then how can you tell they are free in home?
I'm damn sure, that they can manage the office work,
But you can't manage home!
I'm sure!
The society still suppressing women,
Still make their life as a critical one,
Society only leads to the fall of women!
According to my point of view!

21. Mariam Oreoluwa Ariwoola

Mariam Oreoluwa Ariwoola is a Nigerian poetess and a writer. She's an educator, imsporator and a motivator. She's a lover of God art and literature. She aspires to change the world with her writing. She's been awarded many certificates for her writings. She's written many poems of her own and has participated in several anthologies. She looks forward to doing and achieving more. Her pen name is Maryam inks.

Aborting dreams

The place we live in determines our dreams
It's either a dream promoter or dream aborter
It's always been a sad thing in my heart that
The society doesn't encourage success of it's people
Of course because of the uncivilized mindset
The society carries no need for education,and development
An educated man has everything and he who teaches one,
Teaches everybody but no the rich to education
One to freedom of expression, experiences is cut short

Development to be made by the capable cut off
The society at some point in life because of ignorance
Because of jealousy sometimes after many capable hands
The only thing I know of that can solve all this
Is only to take off from the heart any talks of the society
And do the wishes of the heart to the society
Then after seeing the rate of the success, they're dazed
The society then has nothing to say than keep quiet
It's a sadening thing to me when you have something to offer
But denied because of some unreasonable reasons
The society hear my call from today you shouldn't hinder
Any able hand disabled,nor render them useless.

22. Johana Miracline SS

Pursuing master's degree in English language, love to explore the world Everyone probably thinks that they are the best because poets teach you to think about everything in a new way, about yourself or the world. Poets have a lot of things going on.

Social life

To be out of stress and pressure and Dominating
To be in calmness and peace without
Something not to be incorporated into
An ideal thought processed with supression
We are also a part of the society and live in it
We are also the voices and voters of it
The one to comfort and understand the situation
No judgement society with the ability to speak out

23. J.Martina

She is a soul of optimistic,who loves to learn new things. She is a budding writer who had co-authored around immense anthologies and also written numerous quotes,poems,articles,short stories in various writing platforms and many of her writings are featured in the official pages of the writing community.She had acclaimed immense recongnitions for participating in many writing competitions conducted by various writing communities.

We and the Society

We are the society,
And the society is we,
We both are inseparable,
A drawback in one among us,
Will create a great impact,
In both of us,
But we are forgetting it,

Without us,there is no society,
First we have to understand this concept,
The rules taking place in the society,
Are the rules created by us,
If you want to live a peaceful life,
You have to live according to the society,
It is not difficult to live according to it,
Ad because we are the ones who created it,
So keep that in mind,
And make yourself free,
To lead a happy,stressful life.

24. Ibrahim hamza shaaba

Ibrahim hamza shaaba is a poet and he was born 16december2003.He has participated in many anthology as a coauthor.He believe in the power of poetry words of words.

Society cure

We just have to conquer
the fear in the pure universe of society
Society cure of thoughts it on us
that make the reflect on we that make up the society
The curing of society is a power within ourselves
we just have to look down the lane of ourselves
Turning our inner power to gigantic strength to defend,
unite the people that makeup the society
**The universe of thoughts is just like a swing of unknown
dealings of unknown universe of how we individuals deals
with the unexplaineable and complex words of universe
called society..**

25. Prabhjot Kaur

She is Prabhjot kaur. She lives in Delhi. She is doing graduation in BA (JMC). She lives a simple and happy life. You can follow her on instagram-@The_journo_prabhjot_kaur/@prabhjotkaur43270

MIRROR OF SOCIETY

Everyone has double face personality,
Enticing of smiling lips on one side,
And intensive demons on another side,
We use to criticize others,
But don't see ourselves,
We all want peace,
But we don't know,
Peace exists in us,
We all want name, fame and money,
But in this race,
We all forgot humanity,
We all talk about change,

Yet play the same game,
We all in vain trying to find name and fame,
It's time to change the game,
If you want to be happy,
Then try to make others happy,
If society starts trolling you,
Then you should starts ignoring them,
It is bitter truth of our society,
No one will be happy,
In your happiness,
So, know yourself, your abilities,
Because no one knows you better than yourself.

26. SHIZA KARIM

Hello! She is SHIZA KARIM from Patna, Bihar. She is a co author of more than 65 anthologies and a compiler of 5 anthologies. Her debut book as a co author is ARMY'S FOREVER based on BTS. She is a little girl with big dreams and aims. She is a devotee of Islam.

Society

Society will judge us
No matter what
If we'll do good
We're lucky
They are envious of our success
If we fail
We deserve it
Say society
Full of weird people
Judging others
Before judging themselves

Their work
Free people and
Bert
Judging people with no sense
Make society
Say
Cover a little
Don't wear this and don't do that
You're a girl, behave yourself
If they arrive home late
They're character less
Where is the hell their right?
So many specs of society
No one is pure here
Dirty and dirty minded people are there.

27. Raisa.X.Dias

Love to read. Have a knack for writing poetries as well as stories. Amateur baker. Like to listen to music and play the violin. Studying to be a nurse.

SOCIETY A HIDDEN PREJUDICE

The pillars of knowledge, were my strength my guide
But the games of politics and manipulation threw me off my
guard
The feelings of hopelessness and despair are all that's left with
me now
Along with all my hopes and dreams that I had once wished
to share.
We all have ambitions and aspirations
Some small, some big, some from childhood, some from the
experience of life
However the mentality of the public and the nuisance of
patriarchy always shielding us from our true goal.
There may be no escape from the discrimination

No assistance whatsoever, but at the end of it all
Lies true dedication and perseverance which drives us to
achieve what we desire
We have to remember that all we have is ourselves
And use all our capabilities to our best.

28. Siddiqui Daniya

Siddiqui Daniya, Her passion is to precept and put colours with full of energy in her World of Art. She always try to learn and now she works as a COH (Chief Operating Head) in INKING HEARTS WRITING COMMUNITY. She Empower herself with new style of teaching technology and express her creativity through Art skills and as well as writing stories, poetries, and lot more.she also worked as Co-Author in many Anthologies.

Rise upto sunshine

Standup and face towards sunshine
speak up towards the righteous.
How society is affecting our capabilities?
then what's does the society means?
Society is nothing
But a true face
Of Indian cultures.
But the society

Is surrounded by
Some evils who
Make it hell.
because of it we loses
Our peace of minds
health environment and everything.
It takes miles to go to upgrade your life as it back before .
And then comes up
the third person,
the hell to judge us.
who they are ?
Why they interfere
in our life Without
Our permission.
There is nothing just
as the question air &
punctures of ballon
towards life .
And just at the end everyone has its own beats of beauty to
nourish themselves .

29. Aqsa shaikh

**Masters in English, an international content writer,
Researcher and English debator at youth parliament**

Self is for society but....

SOCIETY People has consistently says something
About my eyes,
About my height
About my color complexion
About my points of life
About my art , about my objectives, about my dressing
you know why?
because I'm a young girl
society hurt me ordinarily
Society had become modern
so my school was current and rich
Society was choosy
so my college was carefully chosen
Society was prudish
and decided whom I should walk with
Society is narrow minded

and would like to decide whom I should marry
But does society really care
whether I am happy or if I get a profession?
Self is for society but
Society is not for self.

30. Hira Paul

He is a writer who writes from the heart and induced feelings of love, affection and pain. He goes by the pen name The Heart Writes. A Writer who is trying to change a world through the flowing of black ink on white paper. A member of Lions Clubs International, a writer and Law Student in India holds a vision of better world. He has co-authored more than 30+ Anthologies. Read more of what he has fo share follow him over Instagram - @_hirapaul. He wishes to make a change by being a change where the world but waits for someone to move the fallen tree he walks alone with the willpower and pushes it.

Versailles of Culture - An Hypocrite Society's Perspective

I stood alone in the sea of pain,
While you stood there and watched.
You poured in more pain and sufferings,
How could you stand there and let me feel?
Yes, I am there but not for you but for those who favor me.

You are just a living waste, Go Back, "You Alien".
You are an invader to our land and our lives.
How can you say you belong here?
I have been born in these lands, my parents and my
grandparents have been here.
We have seen the lands being made free of foreign
dominance.
We served the men and women got them food and clothes.
We contributed towards the GDP and the Country.
But you don't look like him, your face resembles alinity.
Your language and the way you dress is not same as ours,
How can you call yourselves a part of our land belonging to
our culture?
You seem like an alien to the land, you look like a thief and a
dacoit, You should Go Back.
But how could you say such, I am from here, see my
documents.
I belong to this land, I am here please let me get the
education I want to pursue.
I want to contribute to the society in the best possible way I
can.
See him how he is jailed he was here yesterday you said he is
one of you.

31. Shalini Thakur

Shalini Thakur is a social activist who wants to work for the humankind. She was a Delhi University student. Her research papers have been published in many International Journals. Through her writings, she is contributing towards betterment of the society.

Ideal Society

As the newborn opened their eyes,
Entered in the society of evils and crimes.
Is this the Ideal Society? The child asked,
Where pollution, corruption and wars attacked.
Lack of food, home and nature do effect the society,
But above all remains the service to the humanity.
Bring the change that you want to see in the world,
Being helpful to humankind, the mother exclaimed.
Revolution never comes in a day.
It tooks lots of mind to think in a way.
The Ideal society of positive and calmness,
Will definitely be achieved, with endeavours that harness.

32. Lakshmi Soni

She is a published writer had worked with 50+ anthologies from various publications house . She is a young passionate soul from Orange City , Maharashtra . By her passion she is a writer , poet, an artist , podcaster , speaker and an anchor. She worked with 50+ anthologies till now & her articles also published in Bengal e-newspaper too . You can also listen her on Spotify . She Always try to connect her writings with her reader's feelings . For read more write ups feel free to visit her Instagram profile... @dil_ki_kalm__

Society

May be Society is nothing but a combination of differ minds
here ....
Who may be can't teaches the good but have a lot of cheers
...
Instead of supports they use the taunts ,unfairs ...
If someone in society try to change their ownself the societies
interfare ...

By the constitution everyone having the freedome to choose better life care ...& Live there life by own ...
When we talking on or thinking about the things like Leave - in , Menstrual cycle ,condoms , pads , sexual health issues ,etc. they ashamed us and using taunts, & the shit gossips ..
If the two people's either girl & boy
waiting or talking with each other in their or after coachings times the aunties or peoples in the society even they don't know them uses the weird talk & call us a characterless on.a spots..
I don't know Why the people don't understand...the skin tone, body, & girl or boy is the differ colors , shape , sizes & genders ...it's not a Society's personal issue, property that they judge the peoples
So be you'r kind of own Beauty , own rules ,own paintbrush , pen , write your thoughts & live your life great & crazyfully by your own way..

33. Yog Utpal Kapadia

Yog Kapadia is a 20 year old young boy with carringlots of dreams on his hand, pursuing CMA. Apart from it he loves playing cricket and spending time with friends. And also loves writting poems and love quotes (shayaris) and using music in a leisure time. For him writting is not just pen and paper but his emotions, which doesn't require any kind of buttering or clothing. He just want that the reader relate themselves with his writtings and adore it, so he can create some change in society and world..!!

Boys Don't Cry..

Walking Straight Parents knew and had seen future in past,
That life gonna be not same as it is;
Realized that its gonna be Heartbreakers of love and dreams,
As constant walking straight as blindfoolded.
From the Day you were born You were told not to drop a
water;
Water !! Water !! from your eyes,

U re a boy, and they don't cry.
The Director was assigned to your life,
Although u were the sole responsible;
U were free of limits and restrictions,
But , NO ! U weren't
. Society is the audience as well as Director of your life,
And u re the actor; performs in favour of Society.
Not in favour but in accordance to it.
And in respect of parenting, u walk straight as blindfolded as
society.

34. Akkshaya S.

Akkshaya resides in Tamil Nadu .She is interested in writing poems, short stories.Her write- ups touches the reality and reaches the reader heart. More over she keep the things simple with the quote! "Lesser the words the more reader gets the creative. Let her writing skill glorify her

This Is Height

This is height
Watching people talking about their rights day and night.
Begging at signals , thrown out of their families.
Rapped by people, getting teased easily.
Not getting acceptance in society.
Facing abuse on a daily basis, people hardly show pity.
Stop that shit right away.
Enough now, you just can't betray.
Tears of emotions from their eyes are bleeding.
Many misconceptions towards them are increasing.
Stop putting label,
Rather help them in being stable.

Accept them, give them jobs.

And I'm sure with their great work all our hearts they'll rob.

All they need is an acceptance.

Let's accept them with all our heart and see how it makes a

huge difference.

There's nothing wrong with them.

Just like us, they too are a gem.

35. Juhi Pusadkar

She is 19 year old student... She believes in self confidence.. she loves to write and dance...

Can this be called as society ??

What is this society ?
What you think it is ?
Did we really need to be part of it ?
Well , I guess yes ; We need to be the part of society ,
Because not for to match there standards or be in depression
,

But Yes we should be the part of this cruel society ,
To find ourselves , the real side of us ,
Society gives us the best challenge ever ,
There sarcastic talks makes us to feel confident and
courageous ,

From my point of view ; one should take society as a game
not as hell ,
And should not get depressed but try to face it in there own
ways ,
Believe me , society works as landmines but yeah they helps
us form our own bright side !!

Hope you enjoyed reading the book. If you want to publish your book in free of cost you can contact us via instagram @nisargwrites/@confused_mayank or mail us at nisarg240804@gmail.com/confusedmayank2006@gmail.com !!

THANK YOU FOR GIVING YOUR PRECIOUS TIME !!!